What the Critics Say About FIRST WINTER RAIN

What I am struck by is the depth and openness of Garrison's work, and a sincerity that raises his art high above the playing field of today's tanka in English. I hadn't hoped to find such a wealth of tanka in one book by a single author this season or next! *First Winter Rain* holds a breadth of felt experience you owe to yourself.

—Larry Kimmel, editor of Winfred Press

First Winter Rain is a welcome new poetry collection from a master of the tanka form in English. Between these covers we find individual tanka grouped in 8 themed chapters, where Denis Garrison's poetic virtuosity ranges across passionate love lyrics, strongly resonant tanka of place, and elegiac mood pieces. There are lush poems of peace, despairing poems of war; poems of hopefulness, poems of resignation; Garrison expresses succinctly the yin and yang of life, often within the one tanka:

> I am a speck
> On this rock in this ocean
> Lost in endless space
> But for this puppy I hold
> I am a warm breathing world

Following the individual poems there is a long final chapter of enthralling tanka presented in sets, strings and sequences, within which each piece stands alone and also resonates with the next. There could be no better description of the brilliance of Garrison's work, as showcased in *First Winter Rain*, than this tanka which appears in its first chapter:

These unstrung beads
Each is a work of art by itself
Fragments of a piece
But each a thing of beauty—
They know the snowflake's secret

—Amelia Fielden M.A., translator and poet, Australia

"Wide-ranging in subject matter, restless and probing in their inquiry of the human heart, Denis Garrison's tanka are somewhere near the fulcrum of all his efforts in poetry as editor, poet, and essayist. This generous, good man gifts us all with a lifetime of experience in the highs and lows of a well-traveled soul."
—Michael McClintock, President, Tanka Society of America

Poet, editor and publisher, Denis M. Garrison, is a key contributor to the development of tanka in English. His practical encouragement of other writers is widely recognised and appreciated. *First Winter Rain: Selected Tanka from 2006–2010* charts his personal journey on the tanka pathway with poems that successfully explore the potential of this diminutive genre to capture the essence of all that is of moment to the human heart.
—Beverley George, Editor: *Eucalypt: a tanka journal*

Denis M. Garrison, well known as the publisher of Modern English Tanka Press, is an accomplished poet in his own right. In *First Winter Rain*, he brings together selected tanka to tell a story, a story which looks very much like his own, but which isn't quite autobiography. The poems carry the deep marks of war and tragedy that must of necessity evolve into a keen appreciation for beauty; without beauty there can be no redemption from the horrors of life. Garrison's details are so vivid and so accurate, that I, who also spent my childhood in Iowa and my adulthood in Maryland, can recognize his places without being told. When he travels foreign sands where I have never trod, I am not lost in an alien landscape but find the same vivid attention to detail gives me a visceral view as if I were riding in the backseat of his memories. *First Winter Rain* is proof that tanka is not a hothouse exotic but a thoroughly naturalized American literary form that can thrive in the most demanding environments.

—M. Kei, author of *Slow Motion: The Log of a Chesapeake Bay Skipjack*

Praise for *First Winter Rain* — It's risky to publish 252 poems gathered from the prior five years of composition. With such a high number written in such a short time, chances are that a lot of weak work will sneak through a screening process that still needs fine-tuning. But, this doesn't seem to be the case here. Almost all of his tanka burst with the energy of the everyday and the experimentation of a curious mind.

—George Swede, editor of *Frogpond: The Journal of the Haiku Society of America*, is a poet, editor and educator, the author of 31 collections of poetry.

First Winter Rain

Other Books by Denis M. Garrison:

Port of Call and Other Poems (1975)
Three Odd Tales (2005)
The Brink at Logan Pond (2005)
Eight Shades of Blue (haiku) (2005)
Hidden River: Haiku (2006)
Sailor in the Rain and Other Poems (2007)
Fire Blossoms: The Birth of Haiku Noir (2008)

First Winter Rain

Selected Tanka from 2006–2010

Denis M. Garrison

Introduction by M. Kei

MODERN ENGLISH TANKA PRESS
BALTIMORE, MARYLAND
2010

THE UNEXAMINED LIFE IS NOT WORTH LIVING.

SOCRATES

MODERN ENGLISH TANKA PRESS

P.O. Box 43717, Baltimore, Maryland 21236 USA

www.themetpress.com   publisher@themetpress.com

First Winter Rain: Selected Tanka from 2006–2010

Printed in the United States of America

2010

First Winter Rain: Selected Tanka from 2006–2010
by Denis M. Garrison

Published by Modern English Tanka Press
Baltimore, Maryland USA

ISBN 978-1-935398-21-9

This book is dedicated
with love and gratitude
to my wife, Deborah,
who both fills my toy balloon
and ties a string to it.

Contents

Introduction by M. Kei 7

I.   Unstrung Beads 29

II.   Place Settings 35

III.   The Silent Row of Portraits 51

IV.   A Blood Tide Rising 65

V.   Lessons in Obscenity 75

VI.   Acts & Omissions 83

VII.   The Mirrored Door 99

VIII. Versificatus Te 117

IX.   Tanka in Sets, Strings & Sequences 123

Acknowledgements 153

About the Poet 159

Introduction

I've known Denis Garrison since the spring of 2006. At the time I was an unknown tanka author, lamenting the difficulties of getting published, while he was the editor of *Haiku Harvest*, which published its last issue and folded. Denis was a receptive listener, so we met for lunch in Havre de Grace, a little town on the Chesapeake Bay midway between our respective abodes in Maryland.

We talked about limits and categories, the haiku wars, and the debate over the definition of tanka. He was tired of the wrangling and was in the process of creating a new literary journal, to be named *3x5*, to deliberately obviate those arguments. He was interested in short lyric verse and all serious attempts to adapt and experiment with Japanese forms in English. After that lunch and discussion with many other poets, he became convinced of the need for a new kind of tanka journal. He changed the proposed journal's name to *Modern English Tanka*, and the rest is history. That history is intricately bound up with the man's own poetry, so it is worthwhile to trace it.

Denis was already a writer and experimenter with haiku, cinquains, crystallines, and many other forms and variations of haiku and tanka; he retains to this day an interest in formal forms, and some of them, as they pertain to tanka, can be found in this volume. Above and beyond that, he was receptive to almost any content and approach for tanka. *Modern English Tanka* overflowed with approximately five hundred poems per issue, demonstrating all sorts of possibilities for the form. Admirers were dazzled by the ecumenical magnitude of the publication; critics opined that he should have cut much more than he did.

Emerging poets and well established names published side by side, and the flood of submissions was proof that while a certain kind of tanka was the only thing being published in the late 20th century, it was not by any means the only sort of tanka being written. Frustrated poets everywhere sent their submissions to *Modern English Tanka*. *MET*, with its poetry and articles, threw open the possibilities of tanka in English. Tanka has become increasingly diverse as a result. Old publications have folded and new come into print; editors have changed and new influences have been discovered and rediscovered. Not all developments have lasting value, but the foment in and of itself fosters an environment in which creativity and skill flourish.

MET also published scholarly articles, and various authors (including this one), published a variety of opinions, reviews, research and experimentation in its pages. A major topic of discussion was the relationship between tanka in the West and tanka in Japan. There were two lines of thought: the first felt it was a Japanese form and must be written only after a thorough study of the Japanese masters (most of them long dead); the second that it was now a Western form that must adapt to its new environment.

The central problem for the first point of view was one of translation: how to make the English language, which is very different from Japanese, do the things that Japanese tanka do? In the beginning, no poets working in English were admitted to the hallowed halls of 'real tanka' as represented by the Japanese masters, but over the last few years even ardent Japanophiles have come to acknowledge a handful of Western poets as worthy of reading and study. Yet the unspoken subtext is that they are suitable topics of study because they have thoroughly absorbed the Japanese tradition; in other words, they have been assimilated by the Japanese. Amelia Fielden and Sanford Goldstein—translators, scholars, and poets—have lived, traveled, and/or worked in Japan for extended periods of time and are fluent in the Japanese language. This implies that the only way to write tanka in English is for the poet to 'go native.'

Opposing them were iconoclasts who felt that tanka, like the sonnet and other imported forms, must adapt to its new environment. In other words, tanka must assimilate into English, changing as necessary to integrate into its new environment. They rejected the dead hand of Japanese classicism, and willingly experimented with form and content. They even went so far as to propose that tanka in English was divorced from its parents and comprised a new form altogether—which argument neo-classicists were quick to seize upon and agree with.

Such arguments were soon omitted from public discussions for fear that such views would be reflected in editorial practice, and that 'unreal' Anglophone tanka would not even be called 'tanka', but merely 'free verse,' elbowed aside, ignored, and forgotten. Champions of tanka as an English-language form fiercely resisted what they perceived as efforts to disenfranchise them via definition and argued for a more inclusive understanding of tanka in English.

Time is no doubt on the side of the broader view; many poets and readers are intimidated by the massive erudition demanded by figures such as Robert Wilson, managing editor of *Simply Haiku*, who maintains a strict focus on Japanese tanka as the sole arbiter of the genre. Two possible results can imagined: readers and poets are turned off by the Japan-centric approach and abandon tanka, leaving it as the province of a small, highly sophisticated elite (as was the case with waka before the tanka reforms), or the Japanophiles will be ignored, and the broader tanka, by being more accessible, will permit more readers and poets to participate, and by their participation, define what tanka in English is.

Denis Garrison is on both sides of the argument. Via *MET* he promoted the great diversification of tanka (a diversity that already existed, but in need of a suitable outlet). He also co-authored with Amelia Fielden and Robert Wilson, 'A Definition of the ideal form of traditional tanka written in English.' Universally accepted by those who already agreed with it, those who had argued against it were equally adamant in their positions. The only obvious it effect it seemed to have had (and that was a small one) was to persuade outsiders that tanka was a moribund form which they had no interest in exploring. Unknown (at the time) to the tanka world, gogyohka had been introduced to North America by Enta Kusakabe, and was finding many adherents who reveled in the freedom it offered. By deliberately breaking with tanka's fixed form and classical past, gogyohka writers did not need to waste time in the arguments and researches that marked the second half of the first decade of the 21st century. However, that was invisible to tanka poets at the time.

In 2008, Garrison's MET Press published Andrew Riutta's book, *Cigarette Butts and Lilacs*. This seminal work presented a dramatically different tanka of such obvious merit that no one could argue against it, even though it represented the sort of poetry that was rarely published in the preceding two decades. Thoroughly grounded in the American experience of rural poverty, hardship, and the challenges that beset ordinary people, it was categorically different from the cherry blossoms, kimonos, and Zen musings that had been popular in the Orientalist tanka of the late 20th century. Riutta was neither the first nor the only poet to write (and publish) such things, but early poets of the hard knocks school of tanka had been forgotten.

Denis, via MET Press, published works that reintroduced these pioneers of tanka in English, such as *Jun Fujita, Tanka Pioneer*. Fujita (born in Japan in 1867 and died in the United States in 1944) was a modern poet. Although his limited published works make no mention of the tanka reforms of the Meiji period, his work was utterly free of neo-classicalism and directly engaged his experience in America. He published a book, *Tanka: Poems in Exile* in 1923. His tanka, 'To Elizabeth,' is a masterwork.

> Against the door dead leaves are falling;
> On your window the cobwebs are black.
> Today, I linger alone.
>
> The foot-step?
> A passer-by.

[Garrison, Denis. M., editor. *Jun Fujita, Tanka Pioneer*. MET Press, 2007]

Fujita was followed by other Japanese American and Japanese Canadian poets during the mid-20th century. Their works were collected in journals and books, of which only one still survives, *Sounds from the Unknown*, edited by Lucille Nixon and Tomoe Tana (uncredited).

> At the factory
> Where I work,
> The morning bells are sounding,
>   And again I begin
>   To burn up my life's energy.
>
> —Keiko Echigo

Nixon, Lucille, ed. *Sounds from the Unknown*. Denver, CO: Alan Swallow, 1963.

Japanese poetics has a word to describe the sort of tanka we resort to calling 'neo-classical': *miyabi*. It means 'courtly elegance,' in other words, appealing to the Japanese elite of the Heian period (794–1185 AD) and shortly thereafter. In contemporary English we can sum it up simply as 'good taste.' Some critics have dismissed tanka lacking in *miyabi* as 'uninteresting' and 'irrelevant.' In some cases they deny that they are even poetry. Although *miyabi* is rarely mentioned by name, the elegance and indirection of the classical Japanese poetry is highly admired by contemporary Western poets. *Miyabi* was a major component of the aesthetic that used to be called 'tanka spirit' in English, back before the diversification of tanka publication and the rediscovery of pioneer poets.

A unifying strand runs through the works of Fujita, the Japanese North American poets of the 20th century, and the work of Andrew Riutta: they apply their poetic training to the landscape in which they live and record it in all its harsh beauty. I dubbed this sort of tanka 'American Gothic Tanka' in an article of the same name (*MET 11*). I used Grant Wood's iconic painting, 'American Gothic,' as an example to illustrate the melding of international aesthetics with American traditions to create a vibrant regional art. The same principles appear in tanka today: what Wood did in paint, North American tanka poets do in words.

The 'American Gothic' aesthetic is part of a larger appreciation for 'dreaming room,' an approach that has been repeatedly discovered and described in English, starting with Jun Fujita and continuing through Lucille Nixon and on to the present day. For 21st century tanka in English, 'dreaming room' is a highly desirable quality—and it was Garrison who gave it its current name.

"By 'dreaming room,' I mean some empty space inside

the poem which the reader can fill with his personal experience, from his unique social context. [...] There is another lens through which to look at this same technique: the concept of multivalency. 'Valence' is used in biology to refer to the forces of reaction and interaction and is used in chemistry to refer to the properties of atoms by which they have the power of combination. This informs the use of the adjective, 'ambivalent,' which refers to confusion and uncertainty. So, we use the term 'multivalency' to refer to the property of words to react to one another, interact with one another, to be fungible and suggestive. A multivalent tanka is one with dreaming room. It is a poem which may be read in many different ways, all of them correct. It is this freedom for the reader that we refer to as making the reader a co-creator of the poem. The reader's experiential context determines the true meaning of the poem, for that reader."

Mounted butterfly
Hanging under hardened glass
Floating over cork
Just enough room for your dreams
Meadow breeze . . . a sapphire flash

Garrison, Denis. M. 'Dreaming Room' editorial, *MET 7*. Also available at <http://www.dengary.com/essays/dreamingroom.html>

Dreaming room requires the participation of the reader to make meaning, just as a dancer makes meaning from the directions given by the choreographer. Neither the dancer nor the reader is free to ignore what they have been given but must contribute to it, finding nuances and possibilities that were not obvious at first glance. The multitude of meanings in a good tanka poem are like a kaleidescope in which the separate pieces can be repeatedly shaken into new patterns.

Garrison's work presented in *First Winter Rain* is exactly this kind of poetry: deeply rooted in American soil, it uses Japanese aesthetics not to create a 'Little Japan,' but to see our American world with a keener eye. Japanese aesthetics are not prescriptions telling us *what* to see, but rather, tools that teach us *how* to see. Western poetry has often been didactic with the poet telling the reader what to find, but the Japanese forms do not usually dictate to the reader. Instead they offer a view and let us lose ourselves in it. These tiny poems open vast vistas.

In 'American Gothic Tanka' I discussed how Garrison's 'Iowa poems'—deeply rooted in the soil of Iowa in a time and place not far from the house depicted in the 'American Gothic' painting—illustrate the principle of casting off *miyabi* to grant a clear vision of what is right in front of us. He conjures not the ghosts of dead Japanese courtiers, but the people of his own world, living and dead. Garrison shows us:

> The grain bin
> Where the hired man died
> Razed to the ground
> Already the footpath
> Is filling up with weeds

No Japanese courtier could or would have written such a poem, and there weren't many places such a poem could have been published in the tanka world of the late 20th century. It appeared in the anthology, *While the Light Holds*, published by Magnapoets in 2009. Similar poems appear in his tanka sequence, 'Last Run to Eden,' which appeared in *MET 2*. One of the verses in that sequence especially caught my eye when I first saw it and continues to resonate with me.

> Fading whistles
> And clatter
> Crossing lights blink off
> Iowa at 2 AM
> Is the dark side of the moon

Having spent my childhood in Iowa, it marked me, just as it marked Garrison—and Wood. Andrew Riutta's poems, although taking place in Michigan, share this 'American Gothic' aesthetic, and so do many other poems that depict places from Hawaii to New Jersey to Saskatchewan. Whether other countries have equivalent tanka I cannot say; I am inclined to think it expresses something unique to the North American continent. It blends indigenous and imported aesthetics, just as the continent is now peopled by a mix of indigenous and immigrant peoples.

Up until now, Riutta, Fujita, Kisaburo Konoshima (author of *Hudson*), and the poets of *Sounds from the Unknown* occupied a very small book shelf; *First Winter Rain* is an important addition to this repetoire. It has a unifying aesthetic, and that aesthetic is American Gothic. Given that Garrison has published a wide variety of works over the years, including several collections of his own poetry, the selections for *First Winter Rain* must be seen as a deliberate poetic statement.

> Baking in the sunlight
> Pulling our strength
> Out of the black dirt
> Enduring the summer heat
> Endless rows of corn and I

Maryland summer
Life inside the emerald
Sun-glare or moon-glow,
Jewel tones or minty pastels,
The green is endless . . . endless

Roasting alive
High sun in Tripoli
The meat market air
Shattered by bellows
From the camel *du jour*

All these poems show the American Gothic aesthetic applied not just to his childhood in Iowa, but to his adulthood in Maryland and his residence in other countries. Having been born and spending my childhood in Iowa and my adulthood in Maryland, I can attest to the accuracy of his vision. I know these places. I recognize them as if I had been shown a snapshot of them. The same approach infuses his poems about Libya with the same multivalency; his Tripoli is not exotic and alien, but a place as real to those who live there as the cornfield of Iowa is to its farmer.

Garrison's eye for place extends not only to physical places, but to emotional places as well.

Dad said, "See this ball.
Look, it has two sharp edges."
"But it's round," I said.
We played catch with it awhile
Then he threw it at my head.

Lean back on my arm
Let your honey hair cascade
Over the edge . . .
For that one naked moment
When neither of us can smile

Late night T'aichung
Lanterns sparkle in the lake
On a crimson bridge
My eyes full of beauty
My shoes full of blood

Denis and I have discussed 'shoes full of blood;' it depicts a real event in his life. Like many veterans he carries scars inside his skin where they are invisible to see. The war poems—-although few in number —-are the rare external signs. Even within his love poems, there's a lurking violence:

As I turn her brooch
To read the inscription
The pin draws blood
If she knew she still can hurt me
She would smile

Garrison—a man who looks like Santa Clause with his long white beard, mild round features, suspenders, and belly—gives a hint of something else lurking beneath the surface of his poetry.

Pink-bellied pup
Asleep in my lap
She's so trusting
I sit for awhile
And kid myself she's right

Garrison is fearless when it comes to expressing the darkness inside, but he is not the only poet to address such topics. Sanford Goldstein is equally unflinching, but although he mentions lashing out at his wife and children in his tanka, he does not strike the reader as being a dangerous man. It is impossible to imagine Goldstein standing on a Chinese bridge with his shoes full of blood. On the other hand, it is very possible to imagine Dave Bacharach doing so; his body of work contains some of the most anti-poetic works in the genre. Who else has written a tanka about a dirty urinal? Goldstein and Bacharach are ordinary men who sometimes lose their tempers, but while individual poems might frighten us, the poet's persona does not. By contrast, Garrison's work carries an insidious and recurring thread of suppressed violence. I think what makes these poems—and the poet's persona—so disturbing is the beauty of that violence. We cannot find beauty in a thing unless some part of us loves it.

In spite of the red thread that weaves through Garrison's poems, there is also mercy. Bacharach can show us tenderness, but that is not the same as mercy; tenderness is what we give to those for whom we have affection. Mercy is what we give to those who have no power over us: mercy is what we give to those who fear us.

> The puma's trail
> Reveals a dragging limp
> I unload my rifle—
> The dinner check is paid
> Without the usual banter

> "Things go well,"
> My friend says " . . . Well. Well."
> Adjusting his coat sleeve
> To hide a soiled cuff
> I peer across the street

Hours before dawn
Drinking vodka on the porch
While others sleep
I turn off the light
And give the moth a break

These are the poems of a man who has made peace with his personal demons. He no longer fears them, but he remains fascinated with the esoteric beauty of what they do to us.

The largest, most variegated thread that runs through Garrison's work is love. It appears in all its forms from childhood to decrepitude. Garrison has not lost his faith in love and he appreciates it in all its forms. It is love that redeems the pain (both physical and mental) and makes life worth living, in spite of its inevitable disappointments.

Grandfather
Transforms the sports page
Into a sea-captain's hat—
When the little boy puts it on,
There is the ocean, in his eyes

My darling barfly,
Spandex taut over 'Depends,'
Dry makeup flakes off
When you smile and yet your eyes . . .
Fires smoulder in the ruins

So far inland
The damp sea-scented breeze
Beguiles my startled senses
Why, today at last,
Do your green eyes smile for me?

The sea does not appear as often as the black dirt or green hills of his homeland, but it calls out all the same in its ceaseless, beckoning voice.

It is time for me
To head off to the fantail
For stogies and rum
The sea-breeze blowing through me . . .
Mother Sea counting my time

The sea is in me . . .
There is no place to escape
My mother's rhythms;
On desert plain or mountaintop,
Her moon still calls out to me

Garrison has told me several times how much he envies me for going to sea on a tall ship; yet the sea, as much as he longs for it, is not necessarily a place of happiness and reward.

Ten of us perched
On the tramp ship's railing
Watching the wake
Waiting for some kind of sign
The nine gulls leave first

The last third of the book is devoted to tanka in groups. Short footnotes explain his definitions of set, string, and sequence. The poems often carry a subtitle informing the reader what sort of group it is, e.g., 'a tanka string.' He is not the only poet to follow this convention, a convention that baffles me. One of the core features of tanka is that they show, not tell. Surely the reader can see for herself that it's a group and find the unity that binds it together. Or find something the poet did not see, something equally valid. 'Dreaming room' applies to groups as well as individual poems.

The tanka sequence is ancient; tanka themselves were originally envoys to longer lyric works in Japanese. Once the long forms were pared down to tanka-sized bites, Japanese poets promptly began reassembling them into longer works: poem tales, sequences, linked verse, and more. The extension has continued in English, with a mid-20th century fad for creation of new forms, such as inverted tanka, double tanka, reversed tanka, and the double reversed inverted tanka. Possibilities for the manipulation of syllables and line counts are endless, and Garrison, who retains a love of formal verse, gives us the 'tanka sonnet,' a nonce form composed of three haiku and a tanka, as well as various other forms.

Other writers have used tanka as a stanzaic form, while still others have built it into sequences again. Sanford Goldstein has offered a definition for 'sequence' that requires it to have a beginning, a middle, and an end, resulting in a change in the narrator. This is the same introduction, rising action, and denouement typical of Western prose. It is not surprising that Western authors have drawn on Western traditions in organizing their tanka. Garrison works with other linear forms, such as the string, but he has also worked with non-linear structures.

Classical Japanese tanka poets placed their emphasis on linking with terminology and rules governing the kinds of linkages, where they occurred in the poem, and what sorts of patterns of subjects and styles they could take. The goal was to avoid monotony and rambling by forcing the sequence to advance and vary in a controlled way. So popular was the activity that it resulted the establishment of renga as a significant genre of poetry. Over time the rules governing sequences and multi-author poems became inricate. Structures in Anglophone poems are usually much simpler, and multi-author poems rarely exceed two or three poets.

Garrison has been a pioneer in this area as well. He and Michael McClintock published two anthologies, *The Five Hole Flute: Modern English Tanka in Sets and Sequences* (2006), the first ever book from MET Press and the first in English devoted to the topic, and *The Dreaming Room: Modern English Tanka in Collage and Montage Sets* (2007). *Modern English Tanka* journal published many sequences under his editorship, and he has contributed to the critical discussion surrounding tanka sequences.

The terms used to describe groups of tanka have multiplied and there is no general agreement as to what the terms mean. I use 'sequence' to refer to tanka arranged in a linear format, as compared to shaped tanka, such as Guy Simser's cross-shaped 'North of Superior.' Within the linear forms there is considerable leeway for organization that progresses logically from the beginning to the end; in other words, the difference between a 'sequence' and a 'string' in Goldstein's definition (which Garrison has adopted) is one of degree rather than any fundamental difference in structure.

Although sequences are almost as old as tanka in English (Fujita's 1923 *Tanka: Poems in Exile* is an exquisitely sequenced work), there has not been as much study of the grouping of tanka as compared to the writing of individual tanka. It is noteworthy that many of the poets who work most with tanka in groups are also editors. Garrison, myself, Amelia Fielden, Sanford Goldstein, Randy Brooks, all are editors. (There are exceptions, e.g., Gary LeBel, who, as far as I know, is not an editor.) So far the sequencing of tanka in English has been an editorial problem: the editor must organize the contents of a journal, book or website in a way that is attractive and useful to the reader and presents the poems effectively. The editor must guide the reader through the work; he cannot simply throw a heap of poem cards at the reader and say, "You figure it out."

Editorial choices effect how poems appear and are read; context influences the perception of the poems. *Sixty Sunflowers*, the Tanka Society of America members' 2006–2007 anthology edited by Sanford Goldstein, is a consummate piece of editing; careful juxtaposition has achieved the maximum possible impact for individual poems and a highly readable anthology. Being a members' anthology, where each member who submits is guaranteed at least one poem published, means that there are a number of undistinguished poems in the anthology. Were *Sixty Sunflowers* torn apart, its constituent parts would not hold up as well as the work as a whole.

The editing of the individual poems in the first two-thirds of *First Winter Rain* illustrates Garrison's considerable skill as an editor. Working with groups of poems is never easy. Groups of more than a few tanka swiftly become unwieldy. Assembling a group of poems in a way that gives them all strength by sticking together combined with enough room to breath is difficult. My favorite group in the collection is 'Baltimore,' a tanka string. Baltimore, a city I know well, is accurately depicted in the tanka. I, too, have felt the divine hush of the stacks of the Enoch Pratt Free Library.

Deep in the stacks
At the Enoch Pratt
I sense the ages
Still breathing, intelligent
Pages waiting to be seen

Step by step Garrison leads us through the streets of Baltimore, their beauty, their angst, their winners and their losers, arriving at last at a fund-raising dinner with its pictures of starving children. The final poem sums up all the others: the carpet of snow in the streets becomes the white linen tablecloth; and the commuters leading their lives of quiet desperation are revealed in their banality by the starving children who know what hardship and unhappiness really are.

To me this is a more sophisticated organization than mere 'string' and it satisfies Goldstein's criteria of a beginning, a middle, and an end, with some change along the way. Perhaps the moments in 'Baltimore' do not occur in precise chronological order, but they do depict moments that build logically as they lead us through the vagaries of urban life to peel back the enervated skin and show us what pain really is. Sequences like this one are why I feel it is not especially useful for the poet to label things as 'strings' or 'sets' or 'montages' or anything else; readers will find their own order in them the same as with individual tanka. Labels are for critics who need convenient handles whereby they can pick up ideas and move them around.

Another excellent sequence is 'Give and Take.' Beginning with a tanka about hiding in a storm cellar while a tornado shrieks outside, it ends with the sounds of a circus leaving town. In between, the sequence describes the devastation of the tornado, but the items chosen for description are small: the bodies of hummingbirds and sowbugs under a board.

I am speechless . . .
The dread beauty of the day . . .
My little sister
Who never breathed
Would have known what to say

Tanka, by definition, are autonomous. Each tanka must make sense when separated from its context. It may gain or lose by that separation, but if it collapses entirely, it isn't a tanka. This makes the tanka sequence—in whatever form it occurs—uniquely different from Western long poems composed of stanzas. Because of tanka's autonomy, it is fair to pull individual tanka out of a sequence for examination.

Rose-grey blanket
The same old smog hangs
Over Baltimore
Night shifts in full swing
The predators awaken

Tanka groups can suffer from redundancy, and this is sometimes the case with Garrison. Sequences have no prescribed length; a poet can repeat himself in new words. This usually does not enhance the power of the sequence. Garrison remains strongly tempted by the Western lyric tradition and his latest journal, *Concise Delight*, publishes short poems from both the Asian and Western traditions. His quest to fuse Eastern and Western traditions has been a hallmark of his work for many years and that interest shows clearly in his sequences.

Generally speaking, tanka sequences, regardless of the organizing principle used, do well to avoid redundancy. The same compactness that is typical of the individual tanka should be applied to sequences.

Not all of the groups in *First Winter Rain* satisfy this criterion. The anaphoric sequence 'Heaven and Earth, Horatio' is an example of a Western poem infused with Eastern influence, but is not a true 'tanka sequence.' However, the poem is highly effective and is an excellent example of the power of hybrid forms. To dismiss 'Heaven and Earth, Horatio' as 'not a tanka sequence' is to miss the point of the poem, and indeed, to miss the point of Garrison's work.

Garrison wraps up his groups of tanka with a tanka garland, a form in which the closing tanka is composed by taking a line from each of the previous tanka. This is a fairly loose definition; some garlands require the last verse to be composed of the first line from the first verse, the second line from the second verse, and so on.

The garland's final tanka is a fit ending for the book:

> Past daily alarms
> Just the two of us, together—
> Mindless of the time
> We lie in the sunset silence
> Beneath the old chestnut tree

The most important aspect of *First Winter Rain* is the way in which Garrison has brought together the traditions and innovations of East and West in a strikingly unique poetic voice. The tanka of *First Winter Rain* are the work of a fully developed poet who thoroughly understands and respects his source materials, but who is not overawed by them. He has the courage to experiment, and if those experiments are not always successful, they are still more interesting than those poets who, once they have found something that works, spend the rest of their careers imitating themselves.

First Winter Rain can take its place along side a handful of other significant works that advance tanka as a genre of English-language literature. It is especially important as a landmark in the emergence of tanka as an indigenized form of English poetry. Just as individual tanka must have autonomy so that they make sense even when removed from their intended context, so too must the genre of tanka in English exhibit the same autonomy so that it can—and should—be read independently from its Japanese origin.

~K~

M. Kei
18 July 2010
aboard the Sail Vessel *Kalmar Nyckel*, Yorktown, Virginia

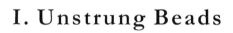

I. Unstrung Beads

Denis M. Garrison

1

My wordless neighbor
Working long after dark
Burying his old hound
The shovel biting the dirt
Like a falling ax

2

Pagliaccio,
You came so close . . . so close
But topsy-turvy!
Take agony for granted—
Then laugh in its bloody face

3

Taking the only piece
Of her mother's fine china
Not yet smashed,
A battered wife
Walks away at dawn

4

Far side of the peak
We pause to pray
Rocking on the waves
Voices of our ancestors
The night wind rising

5

These unstrung beads
Each is a work of art by itself
Fragments of a piece
But each a thing of beauty—
They know the snowflake's secret

II. Place Settings

6

My Iowa
Suffers in the flood
Again! Again!
Not every mile is smooth
But the wheel turns and turns

7

Yet chilled to the bone
I go out for morning chores
A breeze rises with the sun—
The old windmill
Screeches into motion

8

The grain bin
Where the hired man died
Razed to the ground
Already the footpath
Is filling up with weeds

9

August noon
Our barn is blinding red
In from the county road
Floats a summer scent
Hot tar and mown lilies

10

Baking in sunlight
Pulling our strength
Out of the black dirt
Enduring the summer heat
Endless rows of corn and I

11

In the cowshed
Barn cats dance for their milk
Even the runts . . .
The sky goes mauve
And the air grows fragrant

12

Fieldstone spring house
The mossy well burbles
Contentment
There on a hay bale gone soft
Writing my raw-boned verses

13

Maryland summer
Life inside the emerald
Sun-glare or moon-glow,
Jewel tones or minty pastels,
The green is endless . . . endless

14

Raspberry patch
Laced with honeysuckle
Don't mind the thorns
No taste is half so sweet
As that of hard-won fruit

15

The brilliance of a
Susquehanna afternoon
With blinding glitter
The falling sun scatters sparks
Across these rocky shallows

16

Before the race
The dirt track being raked
The rig rattling
Behind a swayback horse
Remembering thunder

17

The hills in autumn's
Red-golden glory are unbowed
This curtain call
After buds and blooms and leaves
Is still one act too soon

18

So far inland
The damp sea-scented breeze
Beguiles my startled senses
Why, today at last,
Do your green eyes smile for me?

19

Through the bare birches
A heavy snow falls in clumps . . .
Their soft landing thumps!
Although the ground's only spotted
Days of silent drifts will come

20

Overnight
The lake ice advanced
Surrounded again
This crumbling bridge . . .
Holding on for vines in spring

21

Again, yellow perch
Running up the Wye
Driven by the moon
Herons and fishermen
Share out the shores, yard by yard

22

More than folk wisdom:
"Every bride is beautiful"
Ah! her rolling curves
Arrayed in snowy blossoms—
These fragrant apple orchards

23

New car smell
In the airport rental . . .
No map clutter
My eyes wide open watching
Scenes unfold around each curve

24

Tenderloin alley
Saturated with old pain
Soaked in suffering
Faded bricks brood in shadow
Even in the noonday sun

25

Flophouse
The darkness of the halls
Mocks flickering lights
Outside, the sun's glare
Waits like a hungry cat

26

The "I" of the eye
Might be anonymous
But the sea it sees
Has an honored name
In every human tongue

27

Silt-choked lake
Full of water hyacinth
Dying shallows—
The sea has deep currents,
Dark places where wild things play

28

Mountain meadow,
The snow-melt trickle runs
Like a lover,
Pell-mell and laughing—
Somewhere, a great river waits

29

Roasting alive
High sun in Tripoli
The meat market air
Shattered by bellows
From the camel *du jour*

30

Where the desert
Pours into the Med
Endless sand meets
Endless sea and, over all,
Empty sky—the sound of wind

31

Gone bruise purple
The southern sky rampant
With simoon
One day in a world of sand
A crash course in erosion

III. The Silent Row of Portraits

32

Newborn
Her tiny helpless hands
Open and close
I kiss them lightly
While they are still pure

33

Early evening
The low sun shines through
All frail things—
The grass, the feeding rabbits,
My brother's hair in gorgeous glow

34

Father, you were
Before ever I drew breath
Now, again, you've gone before
I follow in your trail
From my first home to my last

35

Afloat at last in
My gossamer canoe
Across a darkling deep
Wait for me, Mother,
Beyond the breathing sea

36

Late in the season
The lingering storm breaks
Its gusts snap branches
Winter lightning
Father fights the war, again

37

Tree leaves show
Their silvery undersides
As a storm arrives
I hear the front door slam
Tonight's drama begins . . .

38

Dad said, "See this ball.
Look, it has two sharp edges."
"But it's round," I said.
We played catch with it awhile.
Then he threw it at my head.

39

Dad said "Yin and yang."
I just stared stupidly.
He said "Use and abuse."
And when I sneered he slapped me.
Then he held me tenderly.

40

Leaving home
Without your blessing
Forgive me, Father
This headwind
Is a cold cruel knife

41

The day Grandma died,
In the red glow of Pa's pipe
On the porch that night
For a moment, his wet face—
The one time I saw him weep

42

Holding your last note
Torn, smeared pages, silent in
Empty useless hands
Gone dry and yellow
They curl ... they crumble

43

My father's father
Did the work of ten men
If asked, he'd say,
"When you wake up, get up.
When you get up, do something."

44

My father's workshop
Vacant since his stroke
How quickly even
The finest tools corrode
And lose their cutting edge

45

In my dreams
Dad does chores with me
We work and laugh,
Work and talk . . . but never
Once about the nursing home

46

Drinking hot java
To clear that old boozy fog
I still tightly grip
My chipped "World's Greatest Dad" mug,
Even though it burns . . . it burns

47

Grandfather
Transforms the sports page
Into a sea-captain's hat—
When the little boy puts it on,
There is the ocean, in his eyes

48

He asked me
To bury him when the time came
Not so far away
I said "Yes, of course . . ."
Even now, I see his pale eyes

49

Intensive care
All the chirping monitors
Inconsolable
Song of the cicadas
Rising to a deaf moon

50

I and mine
Struggle on this peak
Together
We are tiring—won't someone
Please throw five lines down

— for Sanford Goldstein

51

I can bear
My elders' graves
But, ah!, the infants
Buried here—their only home—
Leaving, I close the gate with care

52

Time falters
As I walk back to my car
From her new grave—
Chilling, familiar touch!
Fingertips slipping away

53

Spring cleaning
Side by side and cheerfully
We do our chores
Trying hard to forget
The one we lost long ago

54

Unshed tears
I'm told they're high
In calcium . . .
Enough of them, your heart
Can turn to stone

55

You called me
And I followed you
A thousand miles—
Now you have passed over,
Do not fret . . . I will follow

IV. A Blood Tide Rising

56

Forbidden love
My hopeless hunger
For your touch
More secret than
A geisha's blush

57

Peach slices
In thick cream
Luscious
Slick lips tell me
What I want to hear

58

Touch my face
Look into my eyes
Kiss my lips
Mix your heat with mine . . .
Now is all we have

59

Lean back on my arm
Let your honey hair cascade
Over the edge . . .
For that one naked moment
When neither of us can smile

60

Fevered fingers
Coax your enthralled instrument
Tremolo to vibrato
Music swells to your touch
Crescendo in hungry hands

61

The columned arch
Elegant in fire-light
Rises and falls
Wild flames dance
In your half-lidded eyes

62

Pas de deux,
Our blood dances
From allegro to presto
For a passing moment,
I tremble

63

Glistening seaweed
Pulses on the waves
In damp tendrils
Your red-honey hair
Soft on my cheek

Denis M. Garrison

64

Dewy in moonlight
The glistening coral lip
Of the curling wave
Yields to an insistent tide
Surges to the lunar pulse

65

Amid humid hills
After the raging sun's set
Soft crescent shadows
Sweetly deepen to reveal
An orchid gilt by starlight

66

Hands full of heaven
The warm tickle in my palms
Racing through my veins
The serpent in the cellar
Stirs and stretches in the dark

67

Savage beauty
Your face in passion
Something like a cougar's
Growl trembles
Your damp, taut throat

"A POMEGRANATE, OVERRIPE"   *(68–71)*

Come close, young woman,
I'll tell you about onions:
They are the last sum
Of all their layers, oldest
And youngest . . . yes, come closer

    "Tanglewood"
    Splintered and shotgunned
    Welcome sign—
    Your smouldering eyes,
    Scarlet lips and fingertips

        Sandstone garden wall
        Blushes vividly once more
        Warmed by the late light
        Your rouged cheeks and rosacea
        Glow in the winter sunset

            My darling barfly,
            Spandex taut over 'Depends,'
            Dry makeup flakes off
            When you smile and yet your eyes . . .
            Fires smoulder in the ruins

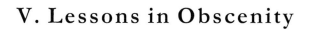

V. Lessons in Obscenity

.

72

A death in summer
The sun eclipsed at noon
A glassy sea
A solemn, silent child
What beast is slouching our way?

73

After the raid
We bury our dead
In the burnt melon field
The littlest graves
Take the longest to dig

74

What does war sound like?
Heavy breathing, furtive footsteps,
Sudden silence, shrieks,
Explosions, huge and small, gunfire,
A grown man's cry for "Mommy!"

75

Deadly April . . .
War rages on, blind to life
Once-greening trees lie around
A tattered lily reflects
In the soldier's still eye

76

Drunks at the bar
Bragging about their combat,
Mowing down enemies . . .
It's easy to tell they lie,
They don't mention the eyes

77

Late night T'aichung
Lanterns sparkle in the lake
On a crimson bridge
My eyes full of beauty
My shoes full of blood

78

Forty years
Are not time enough
To forget
The shouts of "incoming'—
Waking to my own raw voice

79

It is
My barren joy
To have no son
To send away to war . . .
A final wound to wear

80

Why dread
Death's grim frontier?
Youth is mere memory . . .
I have learned the ways of pain
And yearn to know what lies beyond

81

Death be damned!
Mankind is immortal
We know no time
When we were not—
We are dreamers, not the dream

82

This war-shattered city
Roads scattered with bloody glass
Ripe death fills the air
A poet walks weeping streets
A mirror strapped to his back

VI. Acts & Omissions

83

Hold my letter
To your heart,
My kiss today—
Your breast blushes
At the touch of my lips

84

Our love cannot be.
I am not my own—I'll leave
And who'll protect you?
Amongst the ravens, pity
The poor bird that's beautiful.

85

Lush summer meadow
Emeralds in the sun
Sparkle half so green—
When you laugh with the children
I'm lost in your shining eyes

86

Out of the roses
A mammoth redwood rises
A tanager flushes
In ruby-splintered rush
The memory of your smile

87

My fingertips
Sting again with paper cuts
As I count out bills
Paying today's price
For loving you

88

Across the lake
High-rise apartments burn
Flames stab the night sky
When you bark my name
I turn to our latest row

89

For a moment
A jumbo jet taking off
Almost
Drowns out your tirade—
"Say again, my darling?"

90

This parched afternoon
Sparrows bathing in the dust
Do not sing one note
If you should ever return
Don't curse me for my dry eyes

91

Moving house—
There, under my desk,
Your lost photo
Smiling in sweet ignorance
Of cruel days ahead

92

As I turn her brooch
To read the inscription
The pin draws blood
If she knew she still can hurt me
She would smile

93

Moving out at last
I find her bottles stashed
In a secret place
I bury this as well
I cannot mourn for lies

94

Seasons come and go
The lake has changed,
Days are darker now—
Dwindling and loss, yet, I'm rich
With your hand in mine

95

She smoothes
The shoulders of my coat
Her touch familiar
And gentle as dusk
If only I could speak . . .

96

Gripping your wrist
Deafened by falling water
I see only
Your frightened eyes
How long . . . how long?

97

In the long night
In the darkness of grief
Blind to hope
And deaf to prayers
I hold tightly to your hand

98

After all these years
I can hear her eyes speak
When words fail
Made mute by grief, by pain,
I talk by touch

99

As the cold gurney
Shudder-squeaks down the hall
For one more exam
Your hand in mine
Makes us safe

100

Your broken bones
Pain me in a place
Morphine can't reach
I want to take your wounds
But not in trade for mine

101

We smile through tears
And make hopeless plans
As if we had time
One of us is dying
And both of us know

102

You left too soon!
I know you could not stay . . .
I saw the CAT scan
There was so much more to come!
Forgetting, I turn to you . . .

103

The cuckoo clock strikes
I smile at the soft dawn light
Until my eyes rest
On your bare dressing table,
On all the empty hangers

104

Since you left
I sleep very deeply
Alone in our bed—
Good practice, perhaps;
Since coffins sleep only one

105

In the clouds
Your face for a moment
Dissipated by wind
And drunk on sunlight
I call out for you again

106

Empty courtyard
Howls with wind and rain
Hollow desolation—
All night in your chair
Listening for your voice

107

Gone so long
Days pass without
Remembering
Waking to your voice
Calling my name

108

In the park, again
Seated on a board bench
I don't wait long
The stray dog comes for a pet
Then lies at my feet, again

109

The steam whistle's song—
"My dreams are g o n e . . . l o n g   g o n e
Hope's checked out, checked out"
The train lights grow faint, go dark
Vanished into plains of night

VII. The Mirrored Door

110

Does the man
In that mirror
Wonder
What it is like
On the other side?

111

Pink-bellied pup
Asleep in my lap
She's so trusting
I sit still for awhile
And kid myself she's right

112

I am a speck
On this rock in this ocean
Lost in endless space
But for this puppy I hold
I am a warm, breathing world

113

I am still here
Working my sliver of earth—
The oath I swore,
Barefoot on the river stones,
To whispering cottonwoods

114

The clock shop at noon
Cacophony of cuckoos
And various chimes
In time I have learned to love
This discordant melody

115

The puma's trail
Reveals a dragging limp
I unload my rifle—
The dinner check is paid
Without the usual banter

116

Ache,
O, heart of mine—
I am no stone
Hearts have room for joy
But sorrow's in the blood

117

An empty lot
Except these five stone steps
Granite solitude
There is so much to pass on
But no one there to listen

118

Chasing pleasure
I misspent my youth
Joy is free for asking
At last I'm making progress
As a student of suffering

119

My childhood replays
Scenes of sunlit clarity
Over the long years
Since my vision has broadened
To a certain haziness

120

Glancing in my glass
I glimpse my port-red face
No trace of a smile
Is this what the Romans mean
When they say there's truth in wine?

121

Hours before dawn
Drinking vodka on the porch
While others sleep
I turn off the light
And give the moth a break

122

I leave the red cave
Miming dreams in new colors
Sands, hissing like time,
Carve sky towers of blue bone
Where the cold winds come to sing

123

Putting my dog
To sleep . . .
His trusting eyes—
This necessity
Of love

124

Lights on the river
Where the dredges work
Through the night
I drink alone, wondering
Why you had to leave

125

Holy water falls
From the hills in fine white threads;
Green-chalice valley!
Flow through me, mighty river . . .
Receive me, emerald sea

126

Ten of us perched
On the tramp ship's railing
Watching the wake
Waiting for some kind of sign
The nine gulls leave first

127

It is time for me
To head off to the fantail
For stogies and rum
The sea-breeze blowing through me . . .
Mother Sea counting my time

128

Older than language
Heard over both land and sea
Simple eloquence
When written-word's forgotten,
Even then, the cries of gulls . . .

129

The sea is in me . . .
There is no place to escape
My mother's rhythms;
On desert plain or mountaintop,
Her moon still calls out to me

130

Today he returned
After several years' absence
He grasps my hand
So tightly, so long,
I remember why . . .

131

The brief cloud of snow
As an axe strikes this oak
A staggering blow
After his diagnosis
I can't hear the doctor's voice

132

This brisk morning walk
More than by my sweater's warmth
I am comforted
By the crisp chill on my cheeks
By the breezes through my beard

133

Mayflies
You swarm and die
In days—
I will not pity you
I am the childless one

Denis M. Garrison

134

Whose hands are these
Grown graceless, thick and slow?
Not enough fingers,
Too many thumbs to use—
My god, whose face is this?

135

I can't wait for echoes
I am the age of dust
Boundless and drab my emptiness
Yet I tremble
At the touch of living flesh

113

136

Violins, of course,
Can make my heart gently ache
Ah! such sweet laments
Trains at night; their songs pierce me . . .
Haunting horns and endless wheels

137

The moan
Of a passing train
At last
I've learned not to answer
Just because my name is called

138

With my lady wife
I pick my path carefully
In first winter rain
Glory faded, forgotten
Fallen leaves choke the gutters

139

And when
The sand runs out?
The stillness
Of the hourglass
And I are one

VIII. Versificatus Te

140

His hourglass
Passes pencil shavings
Cedar scent
The ageless fragrance
Of the poet's voice

—for Sanford Goldstein, 2008

141

The Mason-Dixon
Family Diner Deluxe
Has paper place mats—
They curl up when my pen
Teases tanka out of them

142

One-penny
Sheet of paper,
Dime pencil,
Half an hour in skilled hands:
The alchemy of words

143

Hammering the wok
Into shape, pounding it out
On the domed anvil;
There is a point when it all
Becomes more about the music

144

Sinuous beauty
Rising off lettered pages
My tanka dragon
Riding on your feathered back
I'm carried to wonder-lands

145

Sleeping poets
Each time eyelids flicker
A poem is born
Hidden in darkness
Bright galaxies bloom

First Winter Rain

146

When Lilith rises
Playing her tenor sax
The world goes green
Stone statues dance and
Butcher-blocks burst into bloom

IX. Tanka in Sets, Strings & Sequences

Denis M. Garrison

BALTIMORE   *(147–157)*

(a tanka string)

To get off
The crowded bus
I shuffle,
Stretch and lean—
The old straphangers' dance

Stepping off
The Trailways bus
At Fayette Street
A chilling rain
The fragrance of diesel

Deep in the stacks
At the Enoch Pratt
I sense the ages
Still breathing, intelligent
Pages waiting to be seen

A National Boh
Sweating on its coaster
Cod cakes catching flies
I'm lost in my newest find
At the Peabody Book Store

First Winter Rain

Lunch at the deli
Next to the fish market
I choose pastrami—
So fine with mustard
And crowds and noise

After working late
In my trudge to the garage
Always this delight—
The moment the sensors click
All the streetlights on at once

Headed north on Charles
In the evening rush hour
Bicyclists pass us by . . .
Inside, my car's AC
Drowns out the daily madness

Downtown
After a late dinner
We step outside
The street is white-carpeted
Snowglobes around each lamppost

Mid-town arcade
Everyone crowds around
The fun-house mirrors . . .
Any illusion will do
For prisoners of reality

"Things go well,"
My friend says ". . . Well. Well."
Adjusting his coat sleeve
To hide a soiled cuff
I peer across the street

Fund-raising dinner
Slides of starving children
Flash quickly by—
The tinkle of crystal
And silver almost stops

"A string is a group of poems that are transitionally connected and focus on a major topic, but there is usually no chronological order, and no conclusion" writes the venerable tanka scholar and poet Sanford Goldstein in his article "Not Again! Yes, Tanka Strings and Tanka Sequences" in the Spring 2010 issue of Atlas Poetica, *No. 5, pg. 60.*

CALIBAN RISING   *(158–165)*

(a tanka sequence)

Sunbeams
Slant upward
From open windows
This cell
Is brightly lit

Six blank walls
The bluestones sing
Echoes from the abyss
Unconsolable shadows
Lurk in the corners

Each time I wake
My bed has moved again
In the dead of night
The cries of songbirds
Come from below

A lover
Soft, warm, wrapped round me
Comforts me
And dispels my terrors
When I wake . . . or when I sleep

Denis M. Garrison

From a window
Of my cell I can see
The rippling backs
Of albatrosses
Soaring high above the waves

The dead things
That I call into being
Disappoint me
Why do they always arrive
Insolent, armed with mischief ?

Where windows were
Mirrors grew, from wall to wall
Vacant bright faces—
Nothing reflects in them
But other mirrors

Outside my walls
I can hear the magma move
Sinking or rising
At last we are on the way
The shadows flicker out

A tanka "sequence" has at least a minimal narrative structure: a beginning, middle, and conclusion. Even in such a surreal group of poems as "Caliban Rising," the narrative progression makes it a "sequence."

GIVE AND TAKE *(166–173)*

(a tanka sequence)

Outside the cellar
A furious tornado shrieks
The air goes thin
We give thanks for safe cover
And a full head count

Topiary art
By power company crews
An ancient elm
Rises around electric lines
Its center never was

I am speechless . . .
The dread beauty of the day . . .
My little sister
Who never breathed
Would have known what to say

Black-green tatters
Of the blasted trumpet vine
Draping the lightning rod
All their tiny bodies,
These silent hummingbirds

Denis M. Garrison

So tired
My arms tremble
A cool breeze
Blows my pain away
Sunlight fills my veins

Under an old board
In my vacant garden plot
The sowbugs thrive—
Religion and politics
Mean less than humidity

Fractured sidewalk
Full of deep green moss
And bulging roots
Those with eyes can see
The garden of eden

A fresh wind
Picks up debris in play
Such clanks and flappings
Our new desert sounds like
The circus leaving town at night

HEAVEN AND EARTH, HORATIO
(174–188)

(an anaphoric triple crown cinquain)

As if
education
over your meager years
and scant experience gave you
clear sight.

As if
your narrow ken,
close measured and approved,
is world enough for you and thus
complete.

As if
the proud, though blind
in their complacency,
by virtue of their rank alone
bear praise.

As if
the humble have
no reason to rejoice—
no kin, no hard-won harvest, and
no dreams.

Denis M. Garrison

As if
mountains never
lurch into the sky, nor
vent the fire within, nor rise from
the sea.

As if
the greening hills
do not stretch and settle
smoothly to attain their soft round
repose.

As if
the creeping vine
does not daily ache for
southern light on the cliff across
the stream.

As if
the flying fish
never throw themselves
above the sea to swim sunlit in
the air.

As if
gannets never
fly beneath the foaming
waves with darting sardine shoals and
dolphins.

First Winter Rain

As if
the zebra mare
forgot her blithe gallops
on the plain or that lions took
her foal.

As if
the howler in
his dotage can't recall
leaping lithely through emerald
treetops.

As if
lemmings stampede
through arctic wilderness
solely for your amusement and
pity.

As if
ten billion squid
in their mating frenzy
care if their misty rite's all right
with you.

As if
your honored chair
is a throne unto all,
and all must orient themselves
to you.

Denis M. Garrison

As if,
Horatio,
the world and all therein
wonder: "How fares Horatio
today?"

The "American Cinquain" is a form created by the Imagist poet and prosodist Adelaide Crapsey, in the early 20th century, as a sort of English tanka. Five-cinquain sequences are called "crown cinquains." This is, I believe, the first triple crown cinquain written. It uses anaphora as its unifying element.

HOW STONE IS MADE *(189–209)*

(a haiku & tanka sequence)

In the city sky
Riding the thermals—
Vultures rise

A still body
On the shattered highway
Shadows of crows

Startled doves
Filling the air above his grave
21 gun salute

Blue spruce forest
The mountain's still scarred
Where wildfire raged—
A man should not
Outlive his son

In the emptiness
You faded away, pale moon—
Merciless white sky

Attending at deathbeds,
Watching their dimming,
Dying eyes—
You can see it when they leave:
We are light

Wind rising—
Kite on a string
Longs to fly

Comforting the kids,
Keeping a stiff upper lip
And a gentle eye,
Letting those, who want to, weep;
Holding my tears for later

Above the dam
Cracked dry mud for miles—
Dust brown willows

Old stand
Of paper birch
Shading the south side
Of a paint-peeling barn
Fluttering in the wind

Brushing snow from her headstone—
A bitter wind rattles
In the trees

First Winter Rain

Knees dusted with snow
The mangroves are still
Waiting for you
House in the clearing . . .
The bed we once shared

Grave-silent
These long nights—
Mute swan in winter

Another new year
And I'm still here waiting
Aching for your voice
Tattered curtains writhe
As the wind claims this ruin

Great oaks creak
In the wind
No birdsong

A chill wind passes
Through windows, doors and halls
The taint of our pain
Echoes of old sorrows
The fireplace moans in the cold

Last year's
New rail fence—
Grey in a still dawn

Denis M. Garrison

Her grave all grassed over—
Missing the touch of her hand,
The brush of her lips;
This phantom pain . . .
It is killing me

Silent bird
Flies south in summer—
Shadow of one swan

On my reed-thatched roof,
The weight of noon sunlight
Presses out the nightmares—
Mouse bones whiten
On the whispering roof

Space for a boulder
Just filled by this boulder—
Trailing orchids

*Combining haiku and tanka in a sequence is really a variation on traditional
Japanese waka poetic practice, but is treated here non-traditionally in a free
structure.*

LAST RUN TO EDEN   *(210–220)*

(a tanka string)

Cold water flat
By the westbound tracks
Shuddering
As car after car
Leaves without me

Even though hundreds
Have passed me by
Each train I'm not on
Seems like
The last run to Eden

Fading whistles
And clatter
Crossing lights blink off
Iowa at 2 AM
Is the dark side of the moon

Westbound at last
All I own in a duffel bag
Breathing different air
I leave far more
Than Iowa behind

Denis M. Garrison

Abandoned tracks
The curve of rusted rails
Into red sunset—
The barmaid's bra
Lies exhausted on the bed

In our pullman berth
We burst out laughing
As our rhythm
Harmonizes
With the racketing rails

Cheerful dining car
Then I notice
Your untouched place setting
The handwritten note
With just one word

At the train station
Waiting on the platform
In case you arrive
A thousand faces pass
Too many but not enough

Outside my window
Million-dollar scenery
For endless miles
I slump in my seat
Your ticket in my fist

First Winter Rain

Heading home
For a funeral of sorts
Riding the rails
Across a golden prairie
Windblown and empty

Night train
Passing in flashes
Your face
For an instant
A dark mirage

Although bits of narrative appear in this tanka string, they are neither connected nor chronological. This string spans a lifetime.

Denis M. Garrison

SECOND WIND   *(221–224)*

(a tanka sonnet)

Rusty hinges
The faded kitchen door
Screeches open

Family album
Its yellow pages brittle
In pallid sunlight
Thin shadows of the dead oak
Scratching at the whitewashed walls

Windows thrown open
Mown grass fragrant wind
Stirs ancient dust

Morning-bright
South facing room
Her cradle will go here

My "tanka sonnet" uses three haiku and one tanka to create a fourteen-line set of poems that resembles the classic sonnet in some respects.

THE DREAMING ROOM   *(225–242)*

(a tanka set)

An azure ceiling
Dangles its yellow parasol
Paper shreds flutter
Like aspen leaves from the beams
As the room goes dark, goes bright

Mounted butterfly
Hanging under hardened glass
Floating over cork
Just enough room for your dreams
Meadow breeze . . . a sapphire flash

The loathsome woods
Do not mean, but be
May the silence
Of the oaks
Abide with thee

I slept in the woods
And the bracken went chestnut
This ancient lake glows
Green at each stroke of my oar
Flocking birds darken the sky

The day's heat broken
My damp shirt cooling, drying
In the tree-row's shade
Red mulberries stain my hands
And the old wooden bucket

This cold white room
Takes on many colors
In the changing light
When will I see you next?
How long until a full moon?

What do I become
In the stupor of the night?
My familiar hands,
What do they conceal by day?
Which nightmare is real; which dream?

Rose-grey blanket
The same old smog hangs
Over Baltimore
Night shifts in full swing
The predators awaken

Skyscrapers sway
Dreaming in the night wind
City's black canyons
Shimmering rivers of light
So faint, the bleats of prey

My ivory dome
Lit by foxfire and coals
The shadows writhe
As my sins flicker
Like dying searchlights

Wet velvet forest
Rooted in the flotsam
Of a sea of tears
The yew-beams of my lodge
Pulse dully in the night

The townsfolk panic
At the sight of painted birds
They raze dark places
And fence-off the forest depths—
Hell arrives in a white van

Rye whisky
Burns my gut, so, cheers!
I've lived so long
An enemy of death
I know pain is proof of life

The doctors insist,
"Lobotomies are painless;
Taking half will leave
Room for happiness, for dreams"—
For whom? Which half am I? Who . . .?

For weeks
After anesthesia
I search
Those hours are nowhere
Like a hole in the sea

Gone are the nightmares
Past are the manic midnights
All's gone sober-grey
Everything tastes like test scores
I dance to the clock's tick-tock

The boy says
He wants to see it all—
Shaking my head
I wonder what he'd do
If the scales fell from his eyes

Some nights
All I can do is lean
Against the old wall
And know
That stone is cold

A tanka "set" has no beginning, middle and conclusion like a tanka "sequence." Its organizational principle may be very subtle—looser even than that of a tanka "string" which usually has a discernible order. An intuitive reader may perceive the underlying wholeness of a tanka "set."

WHEN SHE POURS TEA   *(243–246)*

(a tanka sonnet)

Familiar scent
Steam rising in a twist
Like precious incense

The fault in the glaze,
The petrified drip on the
Smooth rim of the cup,
Reminds my lip that this is
No concept, this is a cup

She seems perfect
Her clothes, her hair just right
The modest smile

Not a single clue
No one else can see
What's killing her

Denis M. Garrison

BEAUTY AT DAY'S END   *(247–252)*

(a tanka garland)

Struggling singles,
Each of us finding our way
Past daily alarms—
Through classes, tests, and schedules,
The dating game, the dreaming

We were a couple,
Just two of us, together—
No one else existed
Our love was like a high wall
Nothing could come between us

Playing with the kids
We never saw the sun's race—
Mindless of the time
We lived *Now* and worshiped *Now*
It came and went like a dream

Tender tangled limbs
Now languid, flushed, slow-moving
Exhausted by our love
Our bodies draped in soft light
We lie in sunset silence

First Winter Rain

Beauty at day's end
Your face in the low warm glow
Youthful in rose light
Beneath the old chestnut tree
That once was younger than we

Past daily alarms
Just two of us, together—
Mindless of the time
We lie in sunset silence
Beneath the old chestnut tree

A "garland" is composed by writing a closing tanka using one line from each of the preceding tanka. This is a technique with its roots in Western poetic practice.

Acknowledgements

These tanka were first published in the venues cited.

"a death in summer" *Twitter,* 2009.
"ache," *Modern English Tanka 5* - Autumn 2007.
"across the lake" *Modern English Tanka 2* - Winter 2006.
"afloat at last in" *Nisqually Delta Review,* Winter/Spring 2007.
"after all these years" *Gusts* #6, Fall/Winter 2007.
"after the raid" *Ribbons* - Spring 2006.
"again, yellow perch" *Concise Delight Poetry* blog, 2009.
"amid humid hills" *Modern English Tanka 3* - Spring 2007.
"an empty lot" *Modern English Tanka 1* - Autumn 2006.
"and when" *Modern English Tanka 5* - Autumn 2007.
"as I turn her brooch" *Fire Pearls* anthology, 2006.
"as the cold gurney" *Fire Pearls* anthology, 2006.
"August noon" *Landfall* anthology, 2007.
"baking in sunlight" *Ribbons* - Autumn 2007.
"before the race" *Twitter,* 2009.
"chasing pleasure" *Modern English Tanka 5* - Autumn 2007.
'come close, young woman," *Modern English Tanka 1* - Autumn 2006.
"Dad said, *see this ball,*" *Modern English Tanka 6* - Winter 2007.
"Dad said *yin and yang . . .*" *Modern English Tanka 6* - Winter 2007.
"deadly April . . ." *Modern English Tanka 5* - Autumn 2007.
"Death be damned!" *Modern English Tanka 8,* Summer 2008.
"dewy in moonlight" *Modern English Tanka 3* - Spring 2007.
"does the man" *Prune Juice #3,* 2009.
'drinking hot java" *Modern English Tanka 7* - Spring 2008.
'drunks at the bar" *Eucalypt 4*, May 2008.
"early evening" *red lights*, January 2010.
"empty courtyard" *Nisqually Delta Review,* Winter/Spring 2006.
'far side of the peak" *Modern English Tanka 7* - Spring 2008.
"father, you were" *Nisqually Delta Review,* Winter/Spring 2007.
"fevered fingers" *Modern English Tanka 3* - Spring 2007.
"fieldstone spring house" *Ribbons* - Autumn 2007.
"flophouse" *Gusts* #6, Fall/Winter 2007.
"for a moment" *Modern English Tanka 4* - Summer 2007.
"forbidden love" *Modern English Tanka 1* - Autumn 2006.
"forty years" *Modern English Tanka 4* - Summer 2007.
"glancing in my glass" *red lights III* - January 2007.
"glistening seaweed" *Tangled Hair* #5 - 2006.
"gone bruise purple" *Atlas Poetica 2*, Autumn 2008

"gone so long" *Modern English Tanka 1* - Autumn 2006.
"grandfather" *Gusts No. 10,* Winter 2009.
"gripping your wrist" *Simply Haiku*, Vol. 4 No. 2, Summer 2006.
"hammering the wok" *Gusts No. 10,* Winter 2009.
"hands full of heaven" *Modern English Tanka 3* - Spring 2007.
"he asked me" *Eucalypt 3*, November 2007.
"his hourglass" *Modern English Tanka 10*, Winter 2008
"hold my letter" *Nisqually Delta Review*, Winter/Spring 2006.
"holding your last note" *Modern English Tanka 2* - Winter 2006.
"holy water falls" *red lights* - Summer 2009.
"hours before dawn" *Modern English Tanka 1* - Autumn 2006.
"I am a speck" *Gusts* #7, Spring/Summer 2008.
"I am still here" *Landfall* anthology, 2007.
"I and mine" *Modern English Tanka 1* - Autumn 2006.
"I can bear" *Concise Delight Poetry* blog, 2009.
"I can't wait for echoes" *Gusts* #5, Spring 2007.
"I leave the red cave" *Nisqually Delta Review*, Winter/Spring 2007.
"in my dreams" *Modern English Tanka 4* - Summer 2007.
'in the clouds" *Modern English Tanka 1* - Autumn 2006.
'in the cowshed" *Landfall* anthology, 2007.
"in the long night" *Eucalypt 3*, November 2007.
'in the park, again" *Modern English Tanka 10*, Winter 2008
"intensive care" *Eucalypt 1*, November 2006.
"it is" *Modern English Tanka 5* - Autumn 2007.
"it is time for me" *Modern English Tanka 7* - Spring 2008.
"late in the season" *Nisqually Delta Review*, Winter/Spring 2007.
"late night T'aichung" *Modern English Tanka 1* - Autumn 2006.
"lean back on my arm" *Modern English Tanka 1* - Autumn 2006.
"leaving home" *Ribbons* - Summer 2006.
"lights on the river" *Fire Pearls* anthology, 2006.
"lush summer meadow" *Modern English Tanka 7* - Spring 2008.
"Maryland summer" *Modern English Tanka 4* - Summer 2007.
"mayflies" *Modern English Tanka 5* - Autumn 2007.
"more than folk wisdom:" *Modern English Tanka 4* - Summer 2007.
"mountain meadow," *red lights*, January 2010.
"moving house—" *Nisqually Delta Review*, Winter/Spring 2006.
"moving out at last" *Fire Pearls* anthology, 2006.
"my childhood replays" *Nisqually Delta Review*, Winter/Spring 2007.
"my darling barfly," *Modern English Tanka 3* - Spring 2007.
"my father's father" *Modern English Tanka 10*, Winter 2008
"my father's workshop" *Sixty Sunflowers* anthology, 2006-2007.
"my fingertips" *Eucalypt 2*, May 2007.

"my Iowa" *Modern English Tanka 8* - Summer 2008.
"my wordless neighbor" *Gusts* #4, Autumn 2006.
"new car smell" *Ribbons* - Spring 2008.
"newborn" *Prune Juice 1*, Winter 2009.
"older than language" *Magnapoets* Summer 2008.
"one-penny" *Gusts No. 10,* Winter 2009.
"Our love cannot be." *Moonset* - Spring 2006.
"out of the roses" *Nisqually Delta Review*, Summer/Fall 2007.
"overnight" *Gusts* #7, Spring/Summer 2008.
"Pagliaccio," *Modern English Tanka 5* - Autumn 2007.
"pas de deux," *Nisqually Delta Review*, Summer/Fall 2006.
"peach slices" *Fire Pearls* anthology, 2006.
"pink-bellied pup" *Modern English Tanka 1* - Autumn 2006.
"putting my dog" *Modern English Tanka 7* - Spring 2008.
"raspberry patch" *Modern English Tanka 4* - Summer 2007.
"roasting alive" *Atlas Poetica* 2, Autumn 2008
"sandstone garden wall" *Modern English Tanka 3* - Spring 2007.
"savage beauty" *Nisqually Delta Review*, Summer/Fall 2006.
"seasons come and go" *Nisqually Delta Review*, Winter/Spring 2006.
"she smoothes" *Gusts* #5, Spring 2007.
"silt-choked lake" *Nisqually Delta Review*, Winter/Spring 2006.
"since you left" *Nisqually Delta Review*, Winter/Spring 2006.
"sinuous beauty" *Modern English Tanka 7* - Spring 2008.
'sleeping poets" *Modern English Tanka 7* - Spring 2008.
"so far inland" *Nisqually Delta Review*, Winter/Spring 2007.
"spring cleaning" *Magnapoets* Spring/Summer 2009 Anthology
"taking the only piece" *Nisqually Delta Review*, Summer/Fall 2006.
"Tanglewood" *Fire Pearls* anthology, 2006.
"ten of us perched" *Wisteria*, July 2007.
"tenderloin alley" *Modern English Tanka 6* - Winter 2007.
"the brief cloud of snow" *Simply Haiku*, Vol. 4 No. 2, Summer 2006.
"the brilliance of a" *Modern English Tanka 4* - Summer 2007.
"the clock shop at noon" *Modern English Tanka 3* - Spring 2007.
"the columned arch" *Modern English Tanka 10* - Winter 2008
"the cuckoo clock strikes" *Fire Pearls* anthology, 2006.
"the day grandma died," *Modern English Tanka 2* - Winter 2006.
"the grain bin" *Magnapoets* Autumn/Winter 2008 Anthology.
"the hills in autumn's" was previously unpublished.
"the 'I' of the eye" *Modern English Tanka 2* - Winter 2006.
"The Mason-Dixon" *Ribbons* - Autumn 2006.
"the moan" *Gusts* #7, Spring/Summer 2008.
"the puma's trail" *Modern English Tanka 2* - Winter 2006.

"the sea is in me . . ." *Magnapoets* Summer 2008.
"the steam whistle's song" *Ribbons* - Winter 2007.
"these unstrung beads" was previously unpublished.
"this brisk morning walk" *Magnapoets* January 2009.
"this parched afternoon" *Ribbons* - Autumn 2006.
"this war-shattered city" *Nisqually Delta Review*, Summer/Fall 2006.
"through the bare birches" *Magnapoets* January 2009.
"time falters" *Modern English Tanka 8* - Summer 2008.
"today he returned" *Modern English Tanka 2* - Winter 2006.
"touch my face" *red lights* - Summer 2009.
"tree leaves show" *Nisqually Delta Review*, Winter/Spring 2007.
"unshed tears" *Simply Haiku*, Vol. 4 No. 2, Summer 2006.
"violins, of course," *Modern English Tanka 6* - Winter 2007.
"we smile through tears" *Modern English Tanka 1* - Autumn 2006.
"what does war sound like?" *Eucalypt 4*, May 2008.
"when Lilith rises" *Fire Pearls* anthology, 2006.
"where the desert" *Atlas Poetica* 2, Autumn 2008.
"whose hands are these" *Sixty Sunflowers* TSA anthology, 2006-2007.
"why dread" *Modern English Tanka 5* - Autumn 2007.
"With my lady wife" was previously unpublished.
"yet chilled to the bone" *Simply Haiku*, Vol. 4 No. 2, Summer 2006.
"you called me" *Gusts*, Spring 2009.
"you left too soon!" *Nisqually Delta Review*, Summer/Fall 2007.
"your broken bones" *Eucalypt 1*, November 2006.

Tanka in Sets, Strings & Sequences

"*Baltimore*" (a tanka string) was published first in *Streetlights: Poetry of Urban Life in Modern English Tanka,* anthology (Baltimore, MD., Modern English Tanka Press. 2009). The tanka "things go well." was first published in *Gusts* #4, Autumn 2006; and "fund-raising dinner" in *Simply Haiku, Vol. 4 No. 2,* Summer 2006.

"*Caliban Rising*" (a tanka sequence) was published first in *The Dreaming Room: Modern English Tanka in Collage and Montage Sets,* anthology, (Baltimore, MD., Modern English Tanka Press. 2007).

"*Give and Take*" (a tanka sequence) was published first in *The Dreaming Room.*

"Heaven and Earth, Horatio" (an anaphoric triple crown cinquain sequence) was published first in *AMAZE: The Cinquain Journal* #2, Fall & Winter 2002. Later published in *The Brink at Logan Pond* (Lulu Press, Morrisville, North Carolina. May 2005); *The Five-Hole Flute: Modern English Tanka in Sequences and Sets,* anthology (Baltimore, MD., Modern English Tanka Press. 2006); *Sailor in the Rain and Other Poems* (Baltimore, MD., Modern English Tanka Press. 2007).

"How Stone Is Made" (a haiku and tanka sequence) was first published in *Lynx XXI*, 2006. <http://www.ahapoetry.com/ahalynx/212solo.html>; "knees dusted with snow" was later anthologized in *Fire Pearls: Short Masterpieces of the Human Heart.* Ed. M. Kei. (Lulu Press, Morrisville, North Carolina. 2006). The sequence was published again in *The Five-Hole Flute.*

"Last Run to Eden" (a tanka string) was published first in *Modern English Tanka* #2 - Winter 2006, without the final tanka, "night train," which was published by itself in *Sixty Sunflowers* TSA members' anthology, 2006-2007. The string was published again in *The Five-Hole Flute.*

"Second Wind" (a tanka sonnet) was published first in *The Five-Hole Flute.*

"The Dreaming Room" (a tanka set) was published first in *The Dreaming Room* anthology. The following individual tanka: "mounted butterfly", "rose-grey blanket", "rye whisky", "for weeks", "the boy says", and "some nights", were first published in *Modern English Tanka* #3, Spring 2007.

"When She Pours Tea" (a tanka sonnet) was published first in *The Five-Hole Flute.* The individual tanka "the fault in the glaze" first appeared in a different form as "Tea Ceremony" in *Templar Phoenix Literary Review*, Fall & Winter 2001 and was reprinted in *The Brink at Logan Pond.*

"Beauty at Day's End" (a tanka garland) was published first in *Modern English Tanka* #9, Autumn 2008.

Verses numbered 113, 137, 139 & 242 were selections in *Take Five: Best Contemporary Tanka, Vol. 1* (2008); verses numbered 8, 121, 132 & 157 were selections in *Take Five: Best Contemporary Tanka, Vol. 2* (2009) (Modern English Tanka Press, Baltimore, Maryland. 2009 & 2010, respectively).

About the Poet

Denis M. Garrison was born in Iowa. He spent most of his childhood in Japan and his youth in Europe, North Africa, and the western Pacific. He has worn many hats in a varied life: sailor, airman, mechanic, electrician, debt collector, sporting goods salesman, quality control technician, boiler-room operator, bureaucrat, small businessman, priest, poet, editor and publisher. Garrison now lives near Maryland's Chesapeake Bay with his lovely wife, Deborah. In the 1970s, Garrison edited Towson University's literary magazine and taught creative writing for Johns Hopkins University's Free University. He has edited numerous poetry journals and currently edits *Ambrosia: Journal of Fine Haiku* and *Concise Delight Magazine of Short Poetry*. His poetry is published in many print and online journals and in several anthologies. Garrison's other collections of poetry now in print include three haiku collections, *Eight Shades of Blue, Hidden River,* and *Fire Blossoms: The Birth of Haiku Noir,* and the free and formal verse collection, *Sailor in the Rain and Other Poems.* Garrison's personal website is at www.dengary.com.

Also from MODERN ENGLISH TANKA PRESS

Take Five: Best Contemporary Tanka, Volume Two ~ M. Kei, Sanford Goldstein, Patricia Prime, Kala Ramesh, Alexis Rotella, Angela Leuck, Eds.

Double Take: Response Tanka ~ Sonja Arntzen and Naomi Beth Wakan.

Home to Ballygunge: Kolkata Tanka ~ William Hart

Black Jack Judy and the Crisco Kids: Bronx Memories ~ Tanka by Alexis Rotella

Where We Go: haiku and tanka sequences and other concise imaginings by Jean LeBlanc.

The Time of This World: 100 tanka from 13 collections by Kawano Yuko, trans. Amelia Fielden & Saeko Ogi.

Peeling an Orange ~ Haiku by Peggy Heinrich. Photographs by John Bolivar.

A Breath of Surrender: A Collection of Recovery-Oriented Haiku ~ Robert Epstein, Ed.

A Poetic Guide to an Ancient Capital: Aizu Yaichi and the City of Nara ~ Michael F. Marra

Elvis In Black Leather ~ Tanka by Alexis Rotella

The Stream Singing Your Name ~ Tanka and Sijo by Jean LeBlanc

Streetlights: Poetry of Urban Life in Modern English Tanka ~ Michael McClintock & Denis M. Garrison, Eds..

Take Five: Best Contemporary Tanka ~ Anthology. M. Kei, Sanford Goldstein, Pamela A. Babusci, Patricia Prime, Bob Lucky & Kala Ramesh, Eds.

All the Horses of Heaven ~ Tanka by James Tipton

Blue Night & the inadequacy of long-stemmed roses / The Temperature of Love (2nd Ed.) ~ Larry Kimmel

Tanka from the Edge ~ Miriam Sagan

Jack Fruit Moon ~ Robert D. Wilson

Meals at Midnight ~ Poems by Michael McClintock

Lilacs After Winter ~ Francis Masat

Proposing to the Woman in the Rear View Mirror ~ Haiku & Senryu by James Tipton.

Abacus: Prose poems, haibun & short poems ~ Gary LeBel

Looking for a Prince: a collection of senryu and kyoka ~ Alexis Rotella

The Tanka Prose Anthology ~ Jeffrey Woodward, Ed.

Greetings from Luna Park ~ Sedoka, James R. Burns

In Two Minds ~ Responsive Tanka by Amelia Fielden and Kathy Kituai

An Unknown Road ~ Haiku by Adelaide B. Shaw

Slow Motion: The Log of a Chesapeake Bay Skipjack ~ M. Kei

Ash Moon Anthology: Poems on Aging in Mod. Engl. Tanka ~ Alexis Rotella & Denis M. Garrison, Eds.

Fire Blossoms: The Birth of Haiku Noir ~ haiku noirs by Denis M. Garrison

Cigarette Butts and Lilacs: tokens of a heritage ~ Tanka by Andrew Riutta

Sailor in the Rain and Other Poems ~ free and formal verse by Denis M. Garrison

Four Decades on My Tanka Road ~ Sanford Goldstein. Fran Witham, Ed.

this hunger, tissue-thin: new & selected tanka 1995–2005 ~ Larry Kimmel

Jun Fujita, Tanka Pioneer ~ Denis M. Garrison, Ed.

Landfall: Poetry of Place in Mod. English Tanka ~ Denis M. Garrison and Michael McClintock, Eds.

Lip Prints: Tanka . . . 1979-2007 ~ Alexis Rotella

Ouch: Senryu That Bite ~ Alexis Rotella

Eavesdropping: Seasonal Haiku ~ Alexis Rotella

Five Lines Down: A Landmark in English Tanka ~ Denis M. Garrison, Ed.

Tanka Teachers Guide ~ Denis M. Garrison, Ed.

Sixty Sunflowers: TSA Members' Anthology 2006-2007 ~ Sanford Goldstein, Ed.

The Dreaming Room: Mod. Engl. Tanka in Collage & Montage Sets ~ M. McClintock & D.M. Garrison, Eds.

The Salesman's Shoes ~ Tanka, James Roderick Burns

Hidden River ~ Haiku by Denis M. Garrison

The Five-Hole Flute: Mod. Engl. Tanka in Sequences & Sets ~ D.M. Garrison & M. McClintock, Eds.

CPSIA information can be obtained at www.ICGtesting.com
Printed in the USA
LVOW100302061011

249333LV00002B/248/P